# HAPPY BIRTHDAY

Published by Stratford Living Publishing.
ISBN Print:978-1-990332-37-1

Dedicated to Grace

# HAPPY BIRTHDAY

# Your Birthay is coming soon!

# And we're planning a Special Surprise for you!

# We hope to keep your Surprise Birthday Party a secret until the day!

# Fingers crossed no one gives the surprise away!

# We made a list of your friends and family...

## Birthday Party GUEST LIST

Mommy, Daddy, Grandma, Auntie, Bobbie, Susan, Carrie, Crystal, Billy, Lance, Perry, Larry, Dana, Harry, Michael, Mitchell, Edgar, Paula.

# And sent them invitations asking them to R-S-V-P!

# Just incase they don't know what that means...

RSVP

# It means YES! On Party Day they are free!

It'll be such a
fabulous day!

BEST
BIRTHDAY
EVER

# And we can't wait to...

# JUMP JUMP JUMP

# AND SAY HAPPY BIRTHDAY TO YOU!

# We hope you'll love the PURPLE THEME!

# Because it's your favourite COLOUR OF THE YEAR!

# EVERYTHING PURPLE...
## - that's our goal!

# We want to celebrate your Birthday with a loud cheer!

# We've asked everyone to wear something with PURPLE in it....

# And to wrap your presents in PURPLE too...

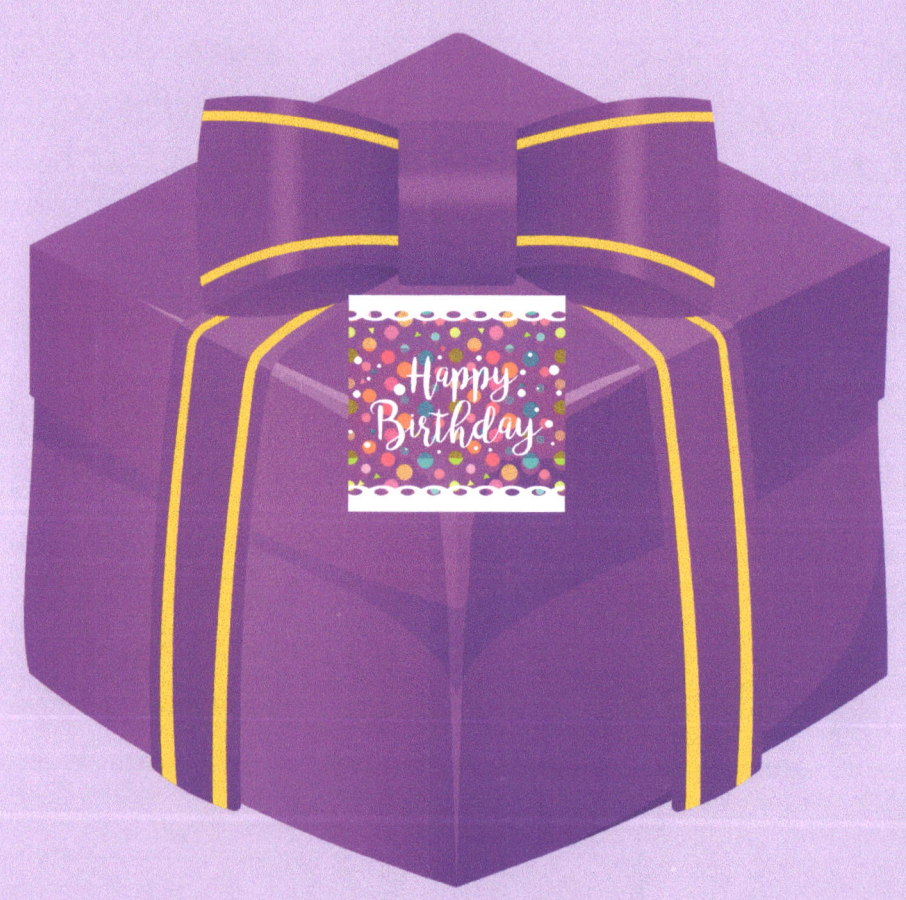

# But we'll have plenty of PURPLE things like HATS ready to help...

# Your Auntie says she might even have a PURPLE HAIRDO!

# We're so excited your Birthday is nearly here!

# We can hardly wait to...

# JUMP JUMP JUMP

# AND SAY HAPPY BIRTHDAY TO YOU!

# Grandma is baking the most amazing PURPLE CAKE!

*Happy Birthday*

# Aunt Stephanie is bringing a PURPLE CAKE PLATE.

# Everyone can have a go at the go at the PURPLE Pinata!

# And the PURPLE JUMPING CASTLE will be great!

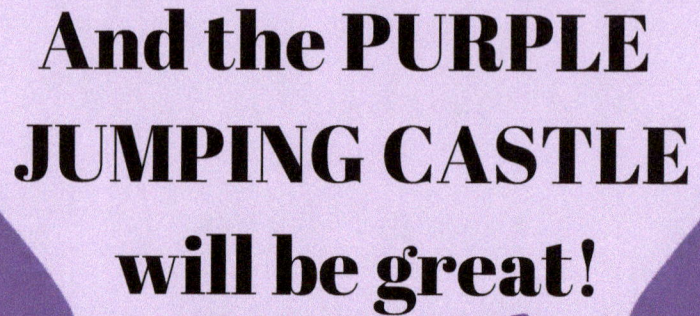

# So, today is finally YOUR BIG DAY!

# We're all quiet and waiting for you to join us!

Happy Birthday

# When you enter we all yell SURPRISE!!!

# And we give your amazed look an A+!

# Now all we have to do is...

# JUMP JUMP JUMP

# AND SING!

# WE

# Birthdays!

Other books in the
Jump Series:
Jump Like a Caribou!
Jump Like a Kangaroo!
Jump at the Zoo!
Jump and Say P.U.!
Jump and Say Boo!
Jump and Say Valentine's Day Is
For Kids Too!
Jump and Look For a Clue
Jump and Say Happy Birthday to You!
Jump For Everything Blue!
Jump and Say Cock-A-Doodle-Do!
Jump and Squawk Like a Cockatoo!
Jump and Ask Is It You or Ewe?

Jump and Say There's an Ewww in My Stew!
Jump and Cheer Happy New Year!
Jump, Hop and Say Happy Easter To You!
Jump and Say There's A Moo-Moo in A Tutu!
Jump and Say There's A Hare in My Hair
Jump and Say My Aunt Ate An Ant!!

The Three Boulders
Billy Shakespeare
Billie Shakespeare

NON-FICTION
103 Fundraising Ideas For Parent Volunteers With Schools and Teams